# contents

Please note that Australian cup and spoon measurements are metric.
A conversion chart appears on page 62.

# gluten-free living

Gluten is a substance found in wheat and other grains and many people are allergic to it. These people have what is called coeliac disease. It's an auto-immune condition that causes damage to the lining of the small intestine when gluten is consumed. The only way to treat it is to avoid wheat, rye, barley and oat products. Symptoms of coeliac disease include fatigue, excessive wind or burping, bloating, stomach cramps and weight gain. See your doctor if you suspect you have coeliac disease and once diagnosed you'll have to resign yourself to a gluten-free life. This might sound daunting at first but as you can see from the recipes in this book, it's not a hardship at all.

**What you can eat**

- fresh fruit, vegetables and herbs
- dairy foods (check labels on ice-creams to be on the safe side)
- beef, pork, lamb, poultry, veal, fish and shellfish
- dried beans, peas, tofu, nuts, rice
- oil, butter and margarine
- rice cakes, rice crackers, popcorn, plain potato chips and corn chips
- tea, coffee, soft drinks, fruit juices.

**What you can't eat**

- wheat, barley, rye, burghul, spelt, malt and oats (some coeliacs are not adversely affected by oats, but until you know for sure, it's wise to avoid them).
- foods made from the above grains – bread, pasta, cereals, pies, biscuits, crackers, cakes and pastries.
- processed food – check labels on all processed foods to make sure it's gluten-free.

Because coeliac disease is so common, and seems to be increasing, most supermarkets now stock quite a range of gluten-free products. All the recipes in this book are made from readily-available products and they've all been triple-tested and tasted by both coeliacs and non-coeliacs. Everyone agreed they're a delicious collection.

# breakfast

## waffles with maple syrup

*This recipe is gluten-free, wheat-free, yeast-free and dairy-free.*

200g dairy-free spread
¾ cup (165g) caster sugar
1 teaspoon vanilla extract
3 eggs, separated
1¼ cups (185g) potato flour
1 cup (200g) brown rice flour
1 teaspoon gluten-free baking powder
1 cup (250ml) water
cooking-oil spray
2 teaspoons pure icing sugar
1 cup (250ml) pure maple syrup

1 Beat spread, caster sugar and extract in medium bowl with electric mixer until light and fluffy. Beat in egg yolks one at a time.
2 Beat egg whites in small bowl with electric mixer until soft peaks form; fold into egg yolk mixture. Fold in sifted dry ingredients and the water. Do not overmix. Mixture may look slightly curdled.
3 Spray heated waffle iron with cooking-oil spray; pour ½ cup batter over bottom element of waffle iron. Close iron; cook waffle about 3 minutes or until browned both sides and crisp. Transfer waffle to plate; cover to keep warm. Repeat with remaining batter, spraying with cooking oil between each one.
4 Serve waffles dusted with sifted icing sugar; drizzle over maple syrup.

**prep + cook time** 45 minutes **makes** 12
**nutritional count per waffle** 15.8g total fat (2.9g saturated fat); 1622kJ (388 cal); 58.1g carbohydrate; 3g protein; 0.8g fibre
**storage** Waffles can be frozen in an airtight container for up to three months. Reheat waffles in the oven.

# gluten-free toasted muesli

*This recipe is gluten-free, wheat-free, yeast-free and egg-free.*

2 tablespoons golden syrup
2 tablespoons macadamia oil
1 cup (50g) gluten-free cornflakes
1 cup (110g) rolled rice
1 cup (20g) puffed rice
1 cup (140g) coarsely chopped macadamias
1 cup (140g) coarsely chopped pistachios
1 cup (160g) coarsely chopped almond kernels
½ cup (25g) flaked coconut
½ cup (100g) finely chopped dried figs
½ cup (65g) dried cranberries

1 Preheat oven to 180°C/160°C fan-forced.
2 Combine syrup and oil in small bowl.
3 Combine cornflakes, rolled rice, puffed rice, nuts and coconut in shallow baking dish; drizzle with syrup mixture. Roast, uncovered, about 15 minutes or until browned lightly, stirring halfway through roasting time. Cool 10 minutes.
4 Stir fruit into muesli mixture; cool.

**prep + cook time** 25 minutes
**makes** 8 cups or serves 24 (⅓ cup per serve)
**nutritional count per serving** 2.7g total fat (2.1g saturated fat); 811kJ (194 cal); 13.5g carbohydrate; 3.7g protein; 2.7g fibre
**storage** Store muesli in an airtight container in the refrigerator for up to one month.

# apple and ricotta fritters

*This recipe is gluten-free, wheat-free and yeast-free.*

1¾ cups (420g) ricotta cheese
⅔ cup (90g) gluten-free self-raising flour
2 tablespoons caster sugar
½ teaspoon ground nutmeg
1 egg
1 large apple (200g), peeled, chopped finely
vegetable oil, for deep-frying
⅓ cup (75g) caster sugar, extra
1 teaspoon ground cinnamon
2 tablespoons pure maple syrup

1 Combine cheese, sifted flour, sugar, nutmeg, egg and apple in medium bowl.
2 Heat oil in large saucepan; deep-fry rounded tablespoons of apple mixture, in batches, until browned lightly. Drain on absorbent paper. Toss fritters in combined extra sugar and cinnamon.
3 Serve fritters drizzled with maple syrup.

**prep + cook time** 25 minutes **makes** 24
**nutritional count per fritter** 3.8g total fat (1.5g saturated fat); 355kJ (85 cal); 10.3g carbohydrate; 2.2g protein; 0.2g fibre

# rolled rice porridge

*This recipe is gluten-free, wheat-free, yeast-free, dairy-free, egg-free and nut-free.*

1½ cups (160g) rolled rice
1.125 litres (4½ cups) water
⅓ cup (80ml) rice milk
⅓ cup (50g) coarsely chopped dried apricots
¼ cup (10g) flaked coconut, toasted
2 tablespoons honey

1 Combine rolled rice and 3 cups of the water in medium bowl. Cover; stand at room temperature overnight.
2 Place undrained rolled rice in medium saucepan; cook, stirring, until mixture comes to the boil. Add the remaining water; return to the boil. Reduce heat; simmer, uncovered, about 5 minutes or until thickened.
3 Divide porridge and milk among serving bowls. Sprinkle with apricots and coconut; drizzle with honey.

**prep + cook time** 20 minutes (+ standing) **serves** 4
**nutritional count per serving** 2.8g total fat (1.7g saturated fat); 1053kJ (252 cal); 50.7g carbohydrate; 3.9g protein; 2.7g fibre
**note** You can substitute the rice milk for soy, whole or skim milk, if you prefer, however, the recipe will no longer be dairy-free if using whole or skim milk.

# banana hotcakes

*This recipe is gluten-free, wheat-free, yeast-free and nut-free.*

1¼ cups (175g) gluten-free self-raising flour
¼ cup (50g) brown rice flour
2 tablespoons caster sugar
1 cup (250ml) milk
3 eggs
40g butter, melted
2 large bananas (460g), sliced thickly
¼ cup (55g) brown sugar

1 Sift flours and sugar into medium bowl. Whisk milk, eggs and half the butter in medium jug. Gradually whisk milk mixture into flour mixture until smooth.
2 Heat large heavy-based frying pan over medium heat; brush with a little of the remaining butter. For each pancake, pour 2 tablespoons batter into heated pan (you can cook three at a time). Cook pancakes until bubbles appear on surface; top pancakes with banana, sprinkle each pancake with a rounded teaspoon of brown sugar. Turn pancakes, cook until sugar has caramelised and banana is browned lightly. Remove from pan; cover to keep warm.
3 Repeat step 2, wiping out pan between batches, to make a total of 12 hotcakes.

**prep + cook time** 25 minutes **makes** 12
**nutritional count per hotcake** 5.1g total fat (2.8g saturated fat); 748kJ (179 cal); 29.3g carbohydrate; 3.3g protein; 0.9g fibre
**note** Accompany with extra fresh sliced banana and maple syrup.

# the lunchbox

## zucchini, olive and tomato polenta fingers

*This recipe is gluten-free, wheat-free, yeast-free, egg-free and nut-free.*

2 cups (500ml) water
2 cups (500ml) gluten-free chicken stock
1 cup (170g) polenta
1 large zucchini (150g), grated coarsely
½ cup (80g) coarsely chopped seeded black olives
⅓ cup (25g) finely grated parmesan cheese
¼ cup (35g) semi-dried tomatoes in oil, drained, chopped finely
2 tablespoons olive oil

1 Oil deep 19cm-square cake pan; line base and sides with baking paper.
2 Bring the water and stock to the boil in large saucepan; gradually stir in polenta. Reduce heat; simmer, stirring, 10 minutes or until polenta thickens. Stir in zucchini, olives, cheese and tomato. Spread polenta mixture into pan; cover, refrigerate about 1 hour or until polenta is firm.
3 Turn polenta onto board; cut in half. Cut each half into six slices.
4 Heat oil in large frying pan; cook polenta until browned both sides.

**prep + cook time** 25 minutes (+ refrigeration)
**makes** 12
**nutritional count per finger** 4.5g total fat (1g saturated fat); 439kJ (105 cal); 12.7g carbohydrate; 2.9g protein; 1.1g fibre
**storage** Cooked polenta fingers can be stored in an airtight container in the refrigerator for up to three days. Polenta fingers can be eaten cold or reheated in the microwave on HIGH (100%) for 30 seconds.

# rice noodle cakes

*This recipe is gluten-free, wheat-free, yeast-free, dairy-free and nut-free.*

200g rice vermicelli noodles
3 eggs, beaten lightly
1 medium carrot (120g), grated coarsely
1 medium zucchini (120g), grated coarsely
½ cup coarsely chopped fresh coriander
2 tablespoons gluten-free sweet chilli sauce
2 tablespoons vegetable oil

1 Place noodles in large heatproof bowl; cover with boiling water. Stand 5 minutes or until tender; drain. Chop noodles coarsely with scissors.
2 Combine noodles, egg, carrot, zucchini, coriander and sauce in large bowl.
3 Heat a little of the oil in large frying pan; pour ¼-cup mixture into pan, flattening slightly with spatula. Cook until browned both sides. Repeat with remaining oil and noodle mixture, cooking three or four cakes at a time.
4 Serve noodle cakes with extra sweet chilli sauce.

**prep + cook time** 35 minutes **makes** 20
**nutritional count per cake** 2.8g total fat (0.5g saturated fat); 263kJ (63 cal); 7.2g carbohydrate; 1.8g protein; 0.5g fibre
**storage** Store cooked rice noodle cakes in an airtight container in the refrigerator for up to three days or freeze for up to three months. Rice noodle cakes can be eaten cold or reheated in the microwave on HIGH (100%) for about 30 seconds.

# omelette wrap

*This recipe is gluten-free, wheat-free, yeast-free and nut-free.*

cooking-oil spray
4 eggs, beaten lightly
2 tablespoons gluten-free mayonnaise
2 teaspoons finely chopped fresh dill
1 teaspoon lemon juice
100g watercress, trimmed
100g smoked salmon
½ lebanese cucumber (65g), seeded, cut into matchsticks

1 Spray medium frying pan with cooking oil; cook half the egg over medium heat, swirling pan to make thin omelette. Remove from pan; cool on baking-paper-covered wire rack. Repeat with remaining egg.
2 Combine mayonnaise, dill and juice in small bowl.
3 Spread each omelette with half the mayonnaise mixture; top with watercress, salmon and cucumber. Roll omelette to enclose filling.

**prep + cook time** 15 minutes (+ cooling) **makes** 2
**nutritional count per wrap** 20.8 total fat (4.5g saturated fat); 1308kJ (313 cal); 5.2g carbohydrate; 25.9g protein; 1.4g fibre
**note** The omelette and mayonnaise mixture can be made the night before and stored, covered, in the refrigerator until ready to assemble the next day.

# pizza pinwheels

*This recipe is gluten-free, wheat-free, yeast-free and nut-free.*

125g butter, softened
1 tablespoon pure icing sugar
2 eggs yolks
1 cup (220g) cooked mashed potato, sieved
1 cup (150g) potato flour
½ cup (80g) brown rice flour
1 tablespoon gluten-free baking powder
⅓ cup (90g) tomato paste
125g gluten-free shaved ham, chopped finely
30g baby spinach leaves
1½ cups (150g) pizza cheese

1 Preheat oven to 220°C/200°C fan-forced. Oil 19cm x 29cm slice pan.
2 Beat butter, sifted sugar and yolks in small bowl with electric mixer until light and fluffy. Transfer mixture to large bowl; stir in mashed potato.
3 Stir in sifted dry ingredients to make a soft dough. Knead dough lightly on floured surface until smooth. Roll dough between sheets of baking paper into a 20cm x 30cm rectangle.
4 Spread tomato paste over dough; sprinkle with ham, spinach and 1 cup of the cheese.
5 Starting from long side, roll dough firmly, using paper as a guide; trim ends. Cut roll into 12 slices; place pinwheels, cut-side up, in single layer, in prepared pan. Bake 20 minutes. Remove pinwheels from oven, sprinkle with remaining cheese; bake further 10 minutes.
6 Serve pinwheels warm or cold.

**prep + cook time** 50 minutes **makes** 12
**nutritional count per pinwheel** 13.4g total fat (8g saturated fat); 961kJ (230 cal); 19.7g carbohydrate; 7.4g protein; 1.1g fibre
**storage** Pinwheels can be stored in an airtight container in the refrigerator overnight, or in the freezer for up to three months.

# indian chickpea and vegetable fritters

*This recipe is gluten-free, wheat-free, yeast-free, egg-free and dairy-free (unless served with yogurt).*

2 cups (300g) chickpea flour
2 large carrots (360g), grated coarsely
1 large brown onion (200g), sliced thinly
1 cup (120g) frozen peas
2 cloves garlic, crushed
1 teaspoon ground cumin
1 teaspoon garam masala
¼ teaspoon ground turmeric
½ teaspoon gluten-free baking powder
⅓ cup coarsely chopped fresh coriander
¼ cup (60ml) water
vegetable oil, for deep-frying

1 Combine ingredients except for oil in medium bowl.
2 Heat oil in wok; deep-fry level tablespoons of vegetable mixture, in batches, until browned lightly and cooked through. Using slotted spoon, remove from pan; drain on absorbent paper.
3 Fritters can be served with natural yogurt.

**prep + cook time** 45 minutes **makes** 36
**nutritional count per fritter** 2g total fat (0.3g saturated fat); 213kJ (51 cal); 5.8g carbohydrate; 2.2g protein; 1.6g fibre
**storage** Fritters can be stored in an airtight container in the refrigerator for up to tree days. Eat fritters cold, or reheat in the microwave on HIGH (100%) for about 20 seconds.

# potato, garlic and oregano pizza

*This recipe is gluten-free, wheat-free, yeast-free, dairy-free and nut-free.*

375g packet gluten-free bread mix
300g baby new potatoes, sliced thinly
2 teaspoons finely chopped fresh oregano
2 teaspoons olive oil
1 clove garlic, crushed

1 Preheat oven to 220°C/200°C fan-forced. Oil two 25cm x 35cm swiss roll pans; line bases with baking paper, extending paper 5cm over long sides.
2 Make bread mix according to packet directions; spread mixture into pans.
3 Combine remaining ingredients in medium bowl; spread potato mixture over bread mix.
4 Bake pizzas about 20 minutes or until potato is tender and bases are crisp.

**prep + cook time** 45 minutes **serves** 6
**nutritional count per serving** 2.3g total fat (0.4g saturated fat); 1116kJ (267 cal); 40.9g carbohydrate; 8.1g protein; 2.8g fibre
**storage** Pizza slices can be stored in an airtight container in the refrigerator for up to two days. Pizza slices can be eaten cold or reheated in the microwave on HIGH (100%) for about 30 seconds.
**note** Baby new potatoes are also known as chats.

# polenta, pancetta and cheese muffins

*This recipe is gluten-free, wheat-free, yeast-free and nut-free.*

1 teaspoon olive oil
200g gluten-free pancetta, chopped finely
4 green onions, sliced thinly
1¼ cups (175g) gluten-free self-raising flour
⅓ cup (55g) polenta
¾ cup (75g) pizza cheese
⅔ cup (160ml) milk
2 eggs
60g butter, melted

1 Preheat oven to 200°C/180°C fan-forced. Line 12-hole (⅓-cup/80ml) muffin pan with paper cases.
2 Heat oil in medium frying pan; cook pancetta, stirring, about 3 minutes or until browned lightly. Add onion; cook, stirring, until soft. Cool.
3 Combine flour, polenta and ½ cup of the cheese in medium bowl; stir in combined milk and eggs, melted butter and pancetta mixture.
4 Divide mixture among paper cases; sprinkle with remaining cheese. Bake, in oven, about 20 minutes. Stand muffins in pan 5 minutes before turning, top-side up, onto wire rack to cool.

**prep + cook time** 35 minutes **makes** 12
**nutritional count per muffin** 9.7g total fat (5.1g saturated fat); 598kJ (143 cal); 16.7g carbohydrate; 7.2g protein; 0.4g fibre
**storage** Muffins can be stored in the refrigerator in an airtight container for up to two days or in the freezer for up to three months.

# egg, bacon and parmesan pies

*This recipe is gluten-free, wheat-free and yeast-free.*

2 teaspoons vegetable oil
3 rindless bacon rashers (195g), chopped finely
1 small brown onion (80g), chopped finely
1 clove garlic, crushed
4 eggs
¼ cup (60ml) cream
¼ cup (20g) finely grated parmesan cheese
1 tablespoon finely chopped fresh chives

### pastry

1 cup (200g) rice flour
¼ cup (35g) (corn) cornflour
¼ cup (30g) soya flour
¼ cup (20g) finely grated parmesan cheese
150g cold butter, chopped
2 tablespoons cold water, approximately

1 Make pastry.
2 Preheat oven to 220°C/200°C fan-forced. Oil six-hole ¾-cup (180ml) texas muffin pan.
3 Roll pastry between sheets of baking paper until 5mm thick; cut six 11cm rounds from pastry. Ease pastry rounds into pan holes, press into base and sides; prick bases with fork.
4 Bake pastry cases about 10 minutes or until browned lightly. Cool cases in pan. Meanwhile, reduce oven temperature to 200°C/180°C fan-forced.
5 Heat oil in small frying pan; cook bacon, onion and garlic, stirring, until bacon is soft. Divide bacon mixture among pastry cases.
6 Whisk eggs and cream in medium jug; stir in cheese and chives. Fill pastry cases with egg mixture. Bake, in oven, about 25 minutes or until mixture is set.
**pastry** Process flours, cheese and butter until fine. Add enough of the water to make ingredients come together. Cover; refrigerate 30 minutes.

**prep + cook time** 50 minutes (+ refrigeration and cooling) **makes** 6
**nutritional count per pie** 37.9g total fat (20.8g saturated fat); 2291kJ (548 cal); 54g carbohydrate; 17.6g protein; 1.5g fibre
**storage** Pies can be stored in an airtight container in the refrigerator for up to three days or in the freezer for up to one month.

# beef lasagne

*This recipe is gluten-free, wheat-free, yeast-free, dairy-free, egg-free and nut-free.*

2 teaspoons olive oil
1 medium brown onion (150g), chopped finely
1 stalk celery (150g), trimmed, chopped finely
1 small zucchini (90g), chopped finely
1 small carrot (70g), chopped finely
2 cloves garlic, crushed
600g beef mince
810g can crushed tomatoes
½ cup (140g) tomato paste
16 x 17cm rice paper squares
1 tablespoon finely chopped fresh chives

white sauce

1½ cups (375ml) water
1 cup (250ml) gluten-free soy milk
2 cloves
1 bay leaf
2 tablespoons dairy-free spread
2 tablespoons (corn) cornflour
100g chive-flavoured soy cheese, chopped coarsely

1 Heat oil in large frying pan; cook onion, celery, zucchini, carrot and garlic until onion is soft. Add beef; cook until changed in colour. Add undrained tomatoes and paste; cook until sauce thickens slightly.

2 Meanwhile, make white sauce.

3 Preheat oven to 180°C/160°C fan-forced. Oil deep 2.5-litre (10-cup) rectangular ovenproof dish.

4 Dip eight rice paper squares, one at a time, into bowl of warm water until soft; place on board covered with tea towel. Spread 1½ cups beef mixture over base of dish; top with soft rice paper. Top with half the remaining beef mixture and half the white sauce.

5 Soften remaining rice paper, place on top of beef mixture; top with remaining beef mixture and white sauce.

6 Bake lasagne about 50 minutes or until browned lightly. Stand 10 minutes; sprinkle with chives before serving.

**white sauce** Boil the water, milk, cloves and bay leaf in saucepan; strain mixture into large heatproof jug, discard solids. Melt spread in same pan; stir in cornflour, cook, 1 minute. Gradually add milk mixture, stirring constantly, until mixture boils and thickens. Stir in cheese.

**prep + cook time** 1 hour 30 minutes
**serves** 6
**nutritional count per serving** 15.2g total fat (4.2g saturated fat); 1484kJ (355 cal); 26.9g carbohydrate; 25.3g protein; 4.5g fibre
**storage** Freeze for up to three months.

# kids' parties

## carrot cupcakes

*This recipe is gluten-free, wheat-free, yeast-free and nut-free. You will need 3 medium carrots (360g) for this recipe.*

⅔ cup (150g) firmly packed brown sugar
½ cup (125ml) vegetable oil
2 eggs
1½ cups (240g) firmly packed coarsely grated carrot
½ cup (75g) potato flour
¼ cup (40g) (corn) cornflour
¼ cup (50g) rice flour
1 teaspoon gluten-free baking powder
¼ teaspoon bicarbonate of soda
1 teaspoon mixed spice
2 x 90g packets coloured gluten-free sugar-free boiled lollies
yellow, pink and orange sugar crystals

cream cheese frosting
125g cream cheese, softened
50g butter, softened
½ cup (80g) pure icing sugar

1 Preheat oven to 180°C/160°C fan-forced. Line 12-hole (⅓-cup/80ml) muffin pan with paper cases.
2 Beat sugar, oil and eggs in small bowl with electric mixer until thick and creamy. Transfer mixture to large bowl; stir in carrot, then sifted dry ingredients. Divide mixture among cases. Bake about 20 minutes; stand 5 minutes, turn, top-side up, onto wire rack to cool.
3 Increase oven temperature to 200°C/180°C fan-forced. Grease oven trays; line with baking paper. Place lollies on trays, in batches of six, about 5cm apart; bake 4 minutes. When cool, lift from trays and mould into petal shapes.
4 Make cream cheese frosting.
5 Spread cakes with three-quarters of the frosting. Position petals on cakes as flowers. Drop remaining frosting into piping bag fitted with a fluted tube; pipe frosting into centre of each flower, sprinkle with sugar crystals.

**cream cheese frosting** Beat cream cheese and butter in small bowl with electric mixer until light and fluffy; gradually beat in sifted sugar.

**prep + cook time** 1 hour **makes** 12
**nutritional count per cupcake** 17.5g total fat (6g saturated fat); 1455kJ (348 cal); 44.9g carbohydrate; 2.5g protein; 0.8g fibre
**storage** Unfrosted cakes can be stored in an airtight container for up to three days, or freeze for up to two months.

# passionfruit and white chocolate jelly cake

*This recipe is gluten-free, wheat-free and yeast-free. You can use any flavoured jelly you like.*

1 teaspoon hazelnut oil
85g packet passionfruit jelly crystals
3 eggs
½ cup (110g) caster sugar
¾ cup (110g) (corn) cornflour
150g white Choc Melts, melted
1m ribbon

**white chocolate ganache**
360g white eating chocolate, chopped coarsely
300ml cream

1 Oil deep 19cm-square cake pan with hazelnut oil. Make jelly according to packet directions; pour into pan. Refrigerate 3 hours or until set.
2 Meanwhile, make white chocolate ganache.
3 Pour three-quarters of the ganache over top of the jelly; refrigerate 1 hour.
4 Meanwhile, preheat oven to 180°C/160°C fan-forced. Grease 23cm-square cake pan; line with baking paper.
5 Beat eggs in small bowl with electric mixer until thick and creamy. Gradually beat in sugar, beating until sugar dissolves. Fold in triple-sifted cornflour. Spread mixture into pan.
6 Bake cake about 20 minutes. Turn cake onto baking-paper-covered wire rack to cool.
7 Trim cake to 19cm-square; place on top of ganache. Refrigerate 30 minutes.
8 Spread chocolate onto baking-paper-lined tray until 3mm thick; refrigerate 10 minutes or until set. Break into small pieces.
9 Place base of pan in sink of hot water for a few seconds to loosen jelly; quickly invert cake onto serving plate. Secure chocolate pieces around edges of cake with remaining ganache; position ribbon.

**white chocolate ganache** Stir chocolate and cream in medium heatproof bowl over medium saucepan of simmering water until smooth. Cool.

**prep + cook time** 40 minutes (+ refrigeration)
**serves** 16
**nutritional count per serving** 20g total fat (12.4g saturated fat); 1413kJ (338 cal); 35.4g carbohydrate; 4.3g protein; 0g fibre
**storage** Cake can be stored, covered, in the refrigerator for up to two days.

# buttercake

*This recipe is gluten-free, wheat-free and yeast-free.*

200g butter, softened
2¼ cups (300g) gluten-free self-raising flour
1 cup (220g) caster sugar
½ cup (125ml) milk
2 eggs
2 egg whites
3 x 10g packets gluten-free edible sugar roses

fluffy frosting
1 cup (220g) caster sugar
½ cup (125ml) water
2 egg whites
green and pink food colouring

1 Preheat oven to 180°C/160°C fan-forced. Grease and line deep 25cm-heart cake pan.
2 Beat butter in medium bowl with electric mixer until changed to a pale colour. Sift flour and ¼ cup of the sugar together. Beat flour mixture and milk into the butter, in two batches, only until combined.
3 Beat eggs and egg whites in small bowl with electric mixer until thick and creamy. Gradually add remaining sugar, one tablespoon at a time, beating until sugar dissolves between additions. With motor operating on low speed, gradually beat egg mixture into flour mixture only until combined.
4 Spread mixture into pan; bake about 50 minutes. Stand cake 10 minutes; turn, top-side up, onto wire rack to cool.
5 Make fluffy frosting. Spread top and sides of cake with pink frosting; decorate cake with roses. Spoon green frosting into small piping bag; pipe leaves onto cake.

**fluffy frosting** Stir sugar and the water in small saucepan over heat, without boiling, until sugar is dissolved. Boil, uncovered, without stirring about 5 minutes or until syrup reaches 116°C on a candy thermometer. Syrup should be thick but not coloured. Remove from heat; allow bubbles to subside. Beat egg whites in small bowl with electric mixer until soft peaks form. While mixer is operating, add hot syrup in a thin stream; beat on high speed about 10 minutes or until mixture is thick and cool. Reserve 2 tablespoons of the frosting in small bowl; tint green. Tint remaining icing pink.

**prep + cook time** 1 hour 15 minutes
**serves** 12
**nutritional count per serving** 15.1g total fat (9.5g saturated fat); 1359kJ (325 cal); 61.4g carbohydrate; 3.1g protein; 0.4g fibre
**storage** Store in an airtight container for up to two days. Undecorated cake can be frozen for up to three months.

# mini meat pies

*This recipe is gluten-free, wheat-free, yeast-free and nut-free.*

2 teaspoons vegetable oil
1 medium brown onion (150g), chopped finely
2 rindless bacon rashers (130g), chopped finely
350g beef mince
2 tablespoons tomato paste
¼ cup (35g) arrowroot
2 cups (500ml) gluten-free beef stock
1 egg, beaten lightly

**pastry**

1¾ cups (350g) rice flour
⅓ cup (50g) (corn) cornflour
⅓ cup (40g) soya flour
200g cold butter, chopped
¼ cup (60ml) cold water, approximately

1 Heat oil in medium saucepan; cook onion and bacon, stirring, until onion softens and bacon is browned. Add beef; cook, stirring, until browned. Add paste and blended arrowroot and stock; bring to the boil stirring. Reduce heat; simmer, uncovered, until mixture is thickened. Cool.

2 Meanwhile, make pastry.

3 Preheat oven to 220°C/200°C fan-forced. Oil 12 x ¼-cup (60ml) foil pie cases (7cm diameter top, 5cm diameter base); place on oven tray.

4 Roll pastry between sheets of baking paper until 5mm thick; cut 12 x 9cm rounds from pastry. Ease pastry rounds into cases; press into base and sides. Spoon beef mixture into pastry cases; brush edges with egg. Cut 12 x 7cm rounds from remaining pastry; place rounds on pies, press pastry to seal edges. Brush pies with remaining egg; cut two small slits in top of each pie.

5 Bake pies about 25 minutes. Serve with gluten-free tomato sauce.

**pastry** Process flours and butter until mixture is fine. Add enough of the water to make ingredients come together. Cover with plastic wrap; refrigerate 30 minutes.

**prep + cook time** 1 hour (+ refrigeration and standing) **makes** 12
**nutritional count per pie** 19.3g total fat (11g saturated fat); 1032kJ (247 cal); 7.8g carbohydrate; 10.7g protein; 0.7g fibre
**storage** Pies can be frozen for up to one month. Reheat defrosted pies in a moderate oven for about 15 minutes.

# mini pizza squares

*This recipe is gluten-free, wheat-free, yeast-free and nut-free.*

375g packet gluten-free bread mix
⅓ cup (90g) tomato paste
2 medium tomatoes (300g), sliced thinly
270g jar char-grilled capsicum in oil, drained, chopped coarsely
½ small red onion (50g), sliced thinly
150g soft fetta cheese, crumbled
440g can pineapple pieces, drained
100g shaved gluten-free ham, chopped coarsely
1 cup (100g) pizza cheese
½ cup (60g) seeded green olives, halved
20 small fresh basil leaves
5 cherry tomatoes (100g), quartered
20 fresh oregano leaves

1 Preheat oven to 220°C/200°C fan-forced. Oil two 25cm x 35cm swiss roll pans; line bases with baking paper, extending paper 5cm over long sides.
2 Make bread mix according to packet directions; press mixture evenly into pans. Bake about 12 minutes or until browned lightly. Remove from oven.
3 Spread paste over bases. Top one pizza base with sliced tomato, capsicum, onion and fetta; top remaining pizza base with pineapple, ham and pizza cheese.
4 Bake pizzas about 15 minutes or until cheese melts and bases are crisp. Cut each pizza into 20 squares. Top capsicum and fetta squares with olives and basil leaves; top ham and pineapple squares with tomato and oregano.

**prep + cook time** 50 minutes
**makes** 40 squares (20 of each pizza)
**nutritional count per capsicum and fetta pizza square** 2.5g total fat (1.2g saturated fat); 284kJ (68 cal); 8.3g carbohydrate; 2.8g protein; 0.7g fibre
**nutritional count per ham and pineapple pizza square** 1.4g total fat (0.8g saturated fat); 272kJ (65 cal); 9.1g carbohydrate; 3.6g protein; 0.8g fibre

# crunchy chicken fingers

*This recipe is gluten-free, wheat-free, yeast-free, dairy-free and nut-free.*

8 chicken tenderloins (600g)
100g packet gluten-free plain potato crisps
1 egg white
⅓ cup (80ml) gluten-free sweet chilli sauce

1 Preheat oven to 200°C/180°C fan-forced.
2 Cut tenderloins in half diagonally.
3 Crush chips coarsely while still in the bag then place in medium shallow bowl. Whisk egg white lightly in small shallow bowl.
4 Dip chicken pieces in egg white then in chips to coat; place, in single layer, on oiled wire rack over oven tray.
5 Bake chicken fingers about 15 minutes or until chicken is cooked through. Serve fingers with sauce.

**prep + cook time** 30 minutes **makes** 16
**nutritional count per finger** 4.2g total fat (1.5g saturated fat); 376kJ (90 cal); 4g carbohydrate; 8.7g protein; 1g fibre
**note** Tomato sauce can be substituted for the sweet chilli sauce.
**storage** Leftover chicken fingers can be kept in the refrigerator for one day, and reheated in the oven.

# mini corn and chive muffins

*This recipe is gluten-free, wheat-free, yeast-free and nut-free.*

1¼ cups (175g) gluten-free self-raising flour
90g butter, melted
2 eggs, beaten lightly
2 x 125g cans gluten-free creamed corn
½ cup (50g) pizza cheese
2 tablespoons finely chopped fresh chives

1 Preheat oven to 200°C/180°C fan-forced. Oil two 12-hole (1-tablespoon/20ml) mini muffin pans.
2 Sift flour into medium bowl; stir in remaining ingredients. Divide mixture among pan holes.
3 Bake muffins about 15 minutes. Stand muffins in pans 5 minutes before turning, top-side up, onto wire rack to cool.

**prep + cook time** 30 minutes **makes** 24
**nutritional count per muffin** 4.1g total fat (2.5g saturated fat); 234kJ (56 cal); 8.1g carbohydrate; 1.5g protein; 0.5g fibre
**storage** Muffins can be stored in an airtight container in the refrigerator for up to two days or in the freezer for up to one month.

# blueberry bubble slice

*This recipe is gluten-free, wheat-free, yeast-free and egg-free.*

180g white eating chocolate, melted
¾ cup (15g) puffed rice
½ cup (40g) desiccated coconut
½ cup (80g) dried blueberries
¼ cup (35g) unsalted pistachios, chopped coarsely

1 Grease 8cm x 26cm bar cake pan; line base and two long sides with baking paper, extending paper 5cm above sides.
2 Combine ingredients in medium bowl. Spoon mixture into pan; refrigerate until set.
3 Remove bubble slice from pan; cut into slices.

**prep + cook time** 15 minutes (+ refrigeration) **makes** 16
**nutritional count per slice** 6.5g total fat (3.9g saturated fat); 405kJ (97 cal); 7.9g carbohydrate; 1.5g protein; 0.7g fibre
**tips** You can substitute the dried blueberries for dried cranberries. Use a serrated knife for cutting the slice.
**storage** Slice can be stored in an airtight container in the refrigerator for up to one week.

# chocolate and fruit crackles

*This recipe is gluten-free, wheat-free, yeast-free, dairy-free and egg-free.*

2 cups (80g) gluten-free cornflakes
1 cup (20g) puffed rice
½ cup (80g) sultanas
⅓ cup (35g) hazelnut meal
2 tablespoons sunflower seeds
250g milk eating chocolate, melted
2 teaspoons gluten-free hundreds and thousands

1 Line two 12-hole (2-tablespoons/40ml) flat-based patty pans with paper cases.
2 Combine cornflakes, puffed rice, sultanas, hazelnut meal and seeds in large bowl; stir in chocolate.
3 Spoon mixture among paper cases, press down gently; sprinkle with hundreds and thousands. Refrigerate 1 hour or until set.

**prep + cook time** 20 minutes (+ refrigeration) **makes** 24
**nutritional count per crackle** 4.4g total fat (1.9g saturated fat); 414kJ (99 cal); 12.6g carbohydrate; 1.7g protein; 0.8g fibre
**storage** Crackles can be stored in an airtight container in the refrigerator for up to one week.

## flourless chocolate hazelnut cake

*This recipe is gluten-free, wheat-free and yeast-free.*

½ cup (50g) cocoa powder
½ cup (125ml) hot water
1½ cups (330g) firmly packed brown sugar
220g unsalted butter, chopped coarsely
200g dark eating chocolate, chopped coarsely
1½ cups (150g) hazelnut meal
6 eggs, beaten lightly
250g strawberries, sliced thinly

**chocolate ganache**
¾ cup (180ml) cream
300g dark eating chocolate, chopped coarsely

1 Preheat oven to 170°C/150°C fan-forced. Grease 25cm-round springform tin; line base and side with baking paper.

2 Blend cocoa with the water in medium saucepan until smooth. Add sugar, butter and chocolate; stir over low heat until smooth. Remove from heat. Stand about 15 minutes or until barely warm. Stir in meal and egg. Pour mixture into tin. Bake about 1 hour 40 minutes. Cool cake in tin. Refrigerate, covered, 3 hours or overnight.

3 Meanwhile, make chocolate ganache. Spread cake with ganache; decorate with strawberries.

**chocolate ganache** Bring cream to the boil in small saucepan. Remove from heat, add chocolate; stir until smooth. Stand 20 minutes before using.

**prep + cook time** 2 hours (+ standing, cooling and refrigeration) **serves** 16

**nutritional count per serving** 33.2g total fat (17.1g saturated fat); 2061kJ (493 cal); 41.6g carbohydrate; 6.7g protein; 1.8g fibre

**tip** This cake is a moist, dense, rich cake. Serve cut into slim wedges.

**storage** Undecorated cake can be stored in an airtight container in the refrigerator for up to one week, or freeze for up to two months.

# orange syrup cake

*This recipe is gluten-free, wheat-free and yeast-free.*

185g butter, softened
1 tablespoon finely grated orange rind
1¼ cups (275g) caster sugar
6 eggs
3 cups (375g) almond meal
¾ cup (60g) desiccated coconut
¾ cup (110g) rice flour
1 teaspoon gluten-free baking powder

### orange syrup

1 large orange (300g)
⅓ cup (75g) caster sugar
⅓ cup (80ml) water

1 Preheat oven to 180°C/160°C fan-forced. Grease 20cm baba cake pan.
2 Beat butter, rind and sugar in medium bowl with electric mixer until light and fluffy. Beat in eggs, one at a time, beating until just combined between additions (mixture will curdle); stir in almond meal, coconut and sifted flour and baking powder. Spread mixture into pan.
3 Bake cake about 1 hour. Stand cake in pan 5 minutes before turning, top-side up, onto wire rack over tray.
4 Meanwhile, make orange syrup; pour hot syrup over hot cake. Serve warm or cold.

**orange syrup** Peel rind thinly from orange; cut into thin strips. Squeeze ⅓ cup juice from orange into small saucepan; add rind, sugar and the water. Stir over heat, without boiling, until sugar dissolves. Simmer, uncovered, without stirring, 10 minutes.

**prep + cook time** 1 hour 40 minutes **serves** 8
**nutritional count per serving** 53.9g total fat (19.7g saturated fat); 3323kJ (795 cal); 59.6g carbohydrate; 16.1g protein; 5.9g fibre
**storage** Store in an airtight container for up to two days. Not suitable to freeze.

# mandarin, polenta and macadamia cake

*This recipe is gluten-free, wheat-free and yeast-free.*

4 small mandarins (400g)
2 cups (280g) macadamias
250g butter, softened
1 teaspoon vanilla extract
1 cup (220g) caster sugar
3 eggs
1 cup (170g) polenta
1 teaspoon gluten-free baking powder
1 tablespoon pure icing sugar

1 Cover whole mandarins in medium saucepan with cold water; bring to the boil. Drain then repeat process twice more. Cool mandarins to room temperature.
2 Preheat oven to 170°C/150°C fan-forced. Grease deep 22cm-round cake pan; line base with baking paper.
3 Blend or process nuts until coarsely ground. Halve mandarins; discard seeds. Blend or process mandarins flesh and rind until pulpy.
4 Beat butter, extract and caster sugar in small bowl with electric mixer until light and fluffy. Beat in eggs, one at a time. Transfer mixture to large bowl; stir in polenta, baking powder, ground nuts and mandarin pulp. Spread mixture into pan.
5 Bake cake about 1 hour. Stand cake in pan 15 minutes; turn, top-side up, onto wire rack to cool. Serve cake dusted with sifted icing sugar.

**prep + cook time** 2 hours 20 minutes (+ cooling time) **serves** 12
**nutritional count per serving** 54.8g total fat (21.1g saturated fat); 3022kJ (795 cal); 49.5g carbohydrate; 7.5g protein; 3.7g fibre
**storage** Store in an airtight container for up to two days, or freeze for up to three months.

# chocolate cake

*This recipe is gluten-free and yeast-free.*
*The cake batter needs to be spread quite thinly to bake properly. If you haven't got two 22cm sandwich pans use two deep 22cm-round cake pans.*

1 cup (125g) soya flour
¾ cup (110g) (corn) cornflour
1¼ teaspoons bicarbonate of soda
½ cup (50g) cocoa powder
1¼ cups (275g) caster sugar
150g butter, melted
1 tablespoon white vinegar
1 cup (250ml) evaporated milk
2 eggs
½ cup mashed banana
2 tablespoons raspberry jam
300ml thickened cream, whipped
2 teaspoons pure icing sugar

1 Preheat oven to 180°C/160°C fan-forced. Grease two 22cm-round sandwich cake pans; line bases with baking paper.
2 Sift flours, soda, cocoa and sugar into large bowl. Add butter, vinegar and milk; beat with electric mixer on low speed for 1 minute. Add eggs, banana and jam; increase speed to medium, beat 2 minutes. Divide mixture between pans.
3 Bake cakes about 30 minutes. Stand cakes in pans 5 minutes before turning, top-side up, onto wire racks to cool.
4 Sandwich cakes with whipped cream; dust with sifted icing sugar.

**prep + cook time** 50 minutes (+ cooling) **serves** 12
**nutritional count per serving** 23.5g total fat (14.8g saturated fat); 1764kJ (422 cal); 42.6g carbohydrate; 9.2g protein; 2g fibre
**note** You need 1 large overripe banana (230g), to get the amount of mashed banana required in this recipe.
**storage** Store in an airtight container for up to two days. Unfilled cake can be frozen for up to three months.

# carrot cake with orange frosting

*This recipe is gluten-free, wheat-free and yeast-free.*

1 cup (125g) soya flour
¾ cup (110g) (corn) cornflour
2 teaspoons gluten-free baking powder
1 teaspoon bicarbonate of soda
2 teaspoons mixed spice
1 cup (220g) firmly packed brown sugar
1½ cups (360g) coarsely grated carrot
1 cup (120g) coarsely chopped walnuts
½ cup (125ml) extra light olive oil
½ cup (120g) sour cream
3 eggs

orange frosting

125g cream cheese, softened
1 teaspoon finely grated orange rind
1½ cups (240g) pure icing sugar

1 Preheat oven to 160°C/140°C fan-forced. Grease deep 20cm-round cake pan; line base and side with baking paper.

2 Sift flours, baking powder, soda and spice into large bowl; stir in sugar, carrot and nuts. Stir in combined oil, sour cream and eggs. Pour mixture into pan.

3 Bake cake 1 hour. Stand cake in pan 5 minutes before turning, top-side up, onto wire rack to cool.

4 Meanwhile, make orange frosting. Top cold cake with frosting.

**orange frosting** Beat cream cheese and rind in small bowl with electric mixer until light and fluffy. Gradually beat in sifted icing sugar until smooth.

**prep + cook time** 1 hour 25 minutes (+ cooling) **serves** 8
**nutritional count per serving** 38.9g total fat (10.7g saturated fat); 3001kJ (718 cal); 80.8g carbohydrate; 10.1g protein; 4.1g fibre
**storage** Store in an airtight container for up to two days. Uniced cake can be frozen for up to three months.

# glossary

**almond meal** also known as ground almonds; powdered to a flour-like texture and used in baking or as a thickening agent.

**arrowroot** a starch made from the rhizome of a Central American plant; used mostly as a thickener.

**bacon rashers** also called bacon slices.

**baking powder** a raising agent; consists of two parts cream of tartar to one part bicarbonate of soda. Gluten-free baking powder is made without cereals.

**bicarbonate of soda** also called baking or carb soda.

**bread mix, gluten-free** a commercial gluten-free bread mix available from most supermarkets.

**butter** use salted or unsalted (sweet); 125g is equal to one stick (4 ounces) butter.

**buttermilk** is commercially made like yogurt; sold alongside dairy products in supermarkets.

**cheese**

**cream** commonly called Philadelphia or Philly; a soft cows-milk cheese with a fat content of at least 33%.

**parmesan** a hard, grainy, cows-milk cheese.

**pizza** a blend of grated mozzarella, cheddar and parmesan cheeses.

**ricotta** a sweet, moist, soft, white, cows-milk cheese; has a slightly grainy texture.

**chicken tenderloins** thin strip under the breast.

**chocolate**

**Choc Melts** small discs of compounded milk, white or dark chocolate; ideal for melting and moulding.

**dark eating** (70% cocoa solids) also called semi-sweet; made of a high percentage of cocoa liquor and cocoa butter, and a little added sugar. We use dark eating chocolate unless stated otherwise.

**white eating** contains no cocoa solids, deriving its sweetness from cocoa butter. Sensitive to heat.

**cocoa powder** also called unsweetened cocoa.

**coriander, fresh** also called cilantro; bright-green-leafed herb with a pungent flavour.

**cornflakes, gluten-free** available from health food stores or the health food section in supermarkets.

**cornflour** (or cornstarch) is used as a thickening agent in cooking;  Available made from wheat or corn. Maize is corn, so whichever word appears on the packet is right for you. It's the "wheat" word you need to avoid.

**cranberries, dried** dried sweetened cranberries.

**cream of tartar** the acid ingredient in baking powder; used in confectionery mixtures to help prevent sugar from crystallising.

**cream** we use pouring cream also known as pure cream.

**sour** thick commercially-cultured sour cream with at least 35% fat content.

**dairy-free spread** (dairy-free margarine) a commercially produced margarine, free of dairy products.

**flour**

**chickpea** also called besan or gram; made from ground chickpeas so is gluten-free and high in protein. Available from health food stores and the health food section in most supermarkets.

**plain** all-purpose flour made from wheat. Also available gluten-free from most major supermarkets.

**potato** made from cooked potatoes that have been dried and ground.

**rice** fine, almost powdery, gluten-free flour; made from ground rice.

**self-raising** plain flour mixed with baking powder in the proportion of 1 cup flour to 2 teaspoons baking powder. Also available gluten-free from most supermarkets.

**soya** made from ground soya beans.

**food colouring** vegetable-based substance available in liquid, paste or gel form.

**garam masala** a blend of ground, roasted spices including fennel, cardamom, cinnamon, cloves, coriander and cumin.

**golden syrup** a by-product of refined sugar cane.

**hazelnut meal** hazelnuts ground to a coarse flour.

**hundreds and thousands** nonpareils; tiny sugar-syrup-coated sugar crystals that come in a variety of bright colours and are used to decorate cakes.

**jelly crystals** a powdered mixture of gelatine, sweetener, and artificial fruit flavouring used to make a moulded, translucent, quivering dessert. Also known as jello.

**mandarin** also called tangerine; a small, loose-skinned, easy-to-peel, sweet and juicy citrus fruit. Mandarin juice is available in the refrigerated section in most supermarkets.

**maple syrup, pure** distilled from the sap of maple trees. Maple-flavoured syrup or pancake syrup is not an adequate substitute for the real thing.

**mixed peel** candied citrus peel.

**mixed spice** a blend of ground spices usually consisting of cinnamon, allspice and nutmeg.

**noodles, rice vermicelli** also called sen mee, mei fun or bee hoon; used in spring rolls and salads. Before using, soak dried noodles in hot water until softened, boil briefly then rinse with hot water.

**oil**

**hazelnut** pressed from crushed hazelnuts.

**macadamia** pressed from ground macadamias. Available in delicatessens and some supermarkets.

**vegetable** from plants rather than animal fats.

**onion**

**green** also called scallion or, incorrectly, shallot; an immature onion picked before the bulb has formed, having a long, bright-green edible stalk.

**red** also called spanish, red spanish or bermuda onion; a sweet-flavoured, large, purple-red onion.

**pancetta** Italian unsmoked bacon; pork belly cured in salt and spices then rolled into a sausage shape and dried for several weeks.

**polenta** also called cornmeal; a flour-like cereal made of corn (maize). Also the dish made from it.

**puffed rice** a breakfast cereal made from rice.

**rice flakes, gluten-free** available from the health food section in most supermarkets.

**rice paper sheets (squares)** also known as banh trang. Made from rice paste and stamped into rounds or squares; stores well at room temperature. Are quite brittle and will break if dropped; dip into water before use.

**rice, rolled** flattened rice grain rolled into flakes; looks similar to rolled oats.

**spinach** also called english spinach and, incorrectly, silver beet.

**sultanas** dried grapes; also known as golden raisins.

**sugar**

**brown** an extremely soft, finely granulated sugar retaining molasses for its colour and flavour.

**caster** also called superfine or finely granulated table sugar. The fine crystals dissolve easily.

**pure icing** also known as confectioners' sugar or powdered sugar; has no added cornflour.

**white** a coarse, granulated table sugar; also called crystal sugar.

**turmeric, ground** also known as kamin; imparts a golden colour to dishes.

**vanilla**

**bean** dried, long, thin pod from a tropical golden orchid; the minuscule black seeds impart a luscious vanilla flavour.

**extract** vanilla beans that have been submerged in water. Vanilla essence is not a suitable substitute.

**watercress** a peppery salad green; highly perishable, so use as soon as possible after purchase.

**zucchini** also known as courgette.

# conversion chart

## MEASURES

One Australian metric measuring cup holds approximately 250ml, one Australian metric tablespoon holds 20ml, one Australian metric teaspoon holds 5ml.

The difference between one country's measuring cups and another's is within a 2- or 3-teaspoon variance, and will not affect your cooking results. North America, New Zealand and the United Kingdom use a 15ml tablespoon. All cup and spoon measurements are level. The most accurate way of measuring dry ingredients is to weigh them. When measuring liquids, use a clear glass or plastic jug with metric markings.

We use large eggs with an average weight of 60g.

## DRY MEASURES

| METRIC | IMPERIAL |
|---|---|
| 15g | ½oz |
| 30g | 1oz |
| 60g | 2oz |
| 90g | 3oz |
| 125g | 4oz (¼lb) |
| 155g | 5oz |
| 185g | 6oz |
| 220g | 7oz |
| 250g | 8oz (½lb) |
| 280g | 9oz |
| 315g | 10oz |
| 345g | 11oz |
| 375g | 12oz (¾lb) |
| 410g | 13oz |
| 440g | 14oz |
| 470g | 15oz |
| 500g | 16oz (1lb) |
| 750g | 24oz (1½lb) |
| 1kg | 32oz (2lb) |

## LIQUID MEASURES

| METRIC | IMPERIAL |
|---|---|
| 30ml | 1 fluid oz |
| 60ml | 2 fluid oz |
| 100ml | 3 fluid oz |
| 125ml | 4 fluid oz |
| 150ml | 5 fluid oz (¼ pint/1 gill) |
| 190ml | 6 fluid oz |
| 250ml | 8 fluid oz |
| 300ml | 10 fluid oz (½ pint) |
| 500ml | 16 fluid oz |
| 600ml | 20 fluid oz (1 pint) |
| 1000ml (1 litre) | 1¾ pints |

## LENGTH MEASURES

| METRIC | IMPERIAL |
|---|---|
| 3mm | ⅛in |
| 6mm | ¼in |
| 1cm | ½in |
| 2cm | ¾in |
| 2.5cm | 1in |
| 5cm | 2in |
| 6cm | 2½in |
| 8cm | 3in |
| 10cm | 4in |
| 13cm | 5in |
| 15cm | 6in |
| 18cm | 7in |
| 20cm | 8in |
| 23cm | 9in |
| 25cm | 10in |
| 28cm | 11in |
| 30cm | 12in (1ft) |

## OVEN TEMPERATURES

These oven temperatures are only a guide for conventional ovens. For fan-forced ovens, check the manufacturer's manual.

| | °C (CELSIUS) | °F (FAHRENHEIT) | GAS MARK |
|---|---|---|---|
| Very slow | 120 | 250 | ½ |
| Slow | 150 | 275-300 | 1-2 |
| Moderately slow | 160 | 325 | 3 |
| Moderate | 180 | 350-375 | 4-5 |
| Moderately hot | 200 | 400 | 6 |
| Hot | 220 | 425-450 | 7-8 |
| Very hot | 240 | 475 | 9 |

# index

**ACP BOOKS**
**General manager** Christine Whiston
**Editor-in-chief** Susan Tomnay
**Creative director** Hieu Chi Nguyen
**Art director + designer** Hannah Blackmore
**Senior editor** Wendy Bryant
**Food writer** Xanthe Roberts
**Food director** Pamela Clark
**Test Kitchen manager + nutritional information** Belinda Farlow
**Sales & rights director** Brian Cearnes
**Marketing manager** Bridget Cody
**Senior business analyst** Rebecca Varela
**Circulation manager** Jarna Mclean
**Operations manager** David Scotto
**Production manager** Victoria Jefferys

ACP Books are published by ACP Magazines
a division of PBL Media Pty Limited
**PBL Media, Chief Executive officer** Ian Law
**Publishing & sales director, Women's lifestyle** Lynette Phillips
**Group editorial director, Women's lifestyle** Pat Ingram
**Marketing director, Women's lifestyle** Matthew Dominello
**Commercial manager, Women's lifestyle** Seymour Cohen
**Research Director, Women's lifestyle** Justin Stone

**Produced by** ACP Books, Sydney.

**Published by** ACP Books, a division of ACP Magazines Ltd, 54 Park St, Sydney; GPO Box 4088, Sydney, NSW 2001.
phone (02) 9282 8618; fax (02) 9267 9438. acpbooks@acpmagazines.com.au; www.acpbooks.com.au

**Printed by** Dai Nippon in Korea.

**Australia** Distributed by Network Services, phone +61 2 9282 8777; fax +61 2 9264 3278;
networkweb@networkservicescompany.com.au
**United Kingdom** Distributed by Australian Consolidated Press (UK), phone (01604) 642 200;
fax (01604) 642 300; books@acpuk.com
**New Zealand** Distributed by Netlink Distribution Company, phone (9) 366 9966; ask@ndc.co.nz
**South Africa** Distributed by PSD Promotions, phone (27 11) 392 6065/6/7;
fax (27 11) 392 6079/80; orders@psdprom.co.za
**Canada** Distributed by Publishers Group Canada
phone (800) 663 5714; fax (800) 565 3770; service@raincoast.com

Title: Gluten-free eating / compiler, Pamela Clark.
ISBN: 978 1 86396 854 6 (pbk.)
Notes: Includes index.
Subjects: Gluten-free diet – Recipes. Gluten-free foods.
Other Authors/Contributors: Clark, Pamela.
Dewey Number: 641.563

ABN 18 053 273 546

**Cover** Carrot cake with orange frosting, page 58
**Photographer** Andre Martin
**Stylist** Sarah O'Brien



**Send recipe enquiries to: recipeenquiries@acpmagazines.com.au**